HARMONIOUS INTERIORS

ROCKPORT

HARMONIOUS INTERIORS

A DESIGN GUIDE FOR CREATING HARMONIOUS ROOMS   ANN McARDLE

GLOUCESTER MASSACHUSETTS

ROCKPORT PUBLISHERS

First published in the United States of America by Rockport Publishers, Inc.
33 Commercial Street
Gloucester, Massachusetts 01930-5089
Telephone: (978) 282-9590
Facsimile: (978) 283-2742
www.rockpub.com

ISBN 1-56496-656-9

10 9 8 7 6 5 4 3 2 1

Cover Image: photographed by Polly Eltes,
courtesy of *Feng Shui for Modern Living*

Credits for photos on pages 6 through 8 can be found on the following pages: 12, 38, 39, 78, 88, and 114 .

Printed in China.

CONTENTS

INTRODUCTION

REFUGE IS INCREASINGLY DIFFICULT TO FIND AS MODERN LIFE IS LIVED AGAINST THE BACKDROP OF FAX MACHINES RINGING, CELL PHONES INTERRUPTING EVERYWHERE WE GO, "YOU'VE GOT MAIL" POPPING UP ON THE COMPUTER SCREEN, AND TRAFFIC JAMS AT ALL HOURS OF THE DAY. THE SANCTUARY THAT HOME CAN PROVIDE BECOMES ESSENTIAL. WE NEED A PLACE TO SHUT OUT THE CACOPHONY OF THE DAY AND LET THE TRAN-QUILITY OF HARMONIOUS SURROUNDINGS REJUVENATE US.

IF YOU HAVE EVER WALKED INTO SOMEONE'S HOME AND AT ONCE EXPERIENCED A FEELING OF COMFORT AND WELL-BEING, YOU KNOW THE MAGIC OF A HARMONIOUS INTERIOR. YEARS AGO, I WENT WITH A FRIEND TO VISIT FRIENDS OF HIS AND WAS IMMEDIATELY AT EASE IN THE HOME OF PEOPLE I HAD JUST MET. THEIR LIBRARY WAS ARCHITEC-TURALLY INVITING—DARK MAHOGANY PANELING OFFSET BY LARGE IRON CASEMENT WINDOWS. THEIR FURNITURE CONSISTED OF A HUGE LEATHER COUCH AND COMFORTABLE, VELVET-UPHOLSTERED SIDE CHAIRS. THERE WERE ACCENTS IN THE CLASSIC MODE: A BUST ON A MAHOGANY TABLE, OLD PRINTS IN DARK FRAMES ON THE WALLS, AN ORIENTAL RUG, AND A CRACKLING FIRE IN THE FIREPLACE. BUT THE QUALITY THAT ENDEARED IT TO ME WAS NOT ITS BEAUTY SO MUCH AS ITS COZY AMBIENCE. THERE WAS NOTHING THAT SEEMED TO BE THERE JUST FOR SHOW. TWO SMALL CHILDREN PLAYED A BOARD GAME ON THE FLOOR; THE ROOM WAS DEFINITELY LIVED-IN. IT ALL LOOKED WELL USED AND LOVED, AND IT BORE THE STAMP OF ITS OWNERS.

IN CHOOSING FURNISHINGS FOR MY NEW LIVING ROOM, I HAVE BEEN GUIDED BY THAT MEMORY. MY SOFA WAS NOT AT ALL WHAT I WAS LOOKING FOR, BUT IT RESONATED WITH ME IN A WAY UNRELATED TO DIMENSION, STYLE, OR COLOR. NOT ONLY DOES IT MAKE THE ROOM LOOK RIGHT, IT HAS TURNED THIS NEW HOUSE INTO MY HOME.

FEEL YOUR REACTION TO ROOMS THAT YOU SEE IN THE HOMES OF YOUR FRIENDS, TO PHOTOGRAPHS IN BOOKS AND MAGAZINES, TO ARTWORK. GET A SENSE OF WHAT KINDS OF FURNISHINGS, WHAT COLORS, WHAT LIGHTING MAKE YOU FEEL RIGHT AND STRIVE FOR THAT IN YOUR OWN HOME. IF FLORALS MAKE YOU FEEL CHEERFUL, USE THEM FOR RUGS, UPHOLSTERY, OR DRAPERY FABRIC. OR USE FLORAL ACCENTS FOR A SMALLER DOSE WITH A SIMILAR IMPACT. IF LEATHER FURNISHINGS AND WOOD PANELING SUIT YOU, CREATE THE MOOD WITH THE RIGHT FABRICS, COLORS, AND TEXTURES. NATURAL WOOD TRIM, OR DARK RATHER THAN WHITE PAINT, MIGHT BE ALL THAT IS NECESSARY. DEEP BROWN, TEXTURED UPHOLSTERY CAN TAKE THE PLACE OF LEATHER AT A FRACTION OF THE COST. YOU CAN GET THE LOOK AND FEEL YOU WANT WITHIN YOUR OWN CONSTRAINTS.

PERFECTION IS NOT THE GOAL. COMFORT, EASE, TRANQUILITY, COMPATIBILITY WITH THE INHABITANTS—THESE ARE THE QUALITIES THAT ENCOMPASS THE IDEA OF A HARMONIOUS INTERIOR. *HARMONIOUS INTERIORS* WILL GUIDE YOUR DECORATING CHOICES TO CREATE A RESTFUL AMBIENCE TO BALANCE YOUR HECTIC LIFE AND BRING YOU A SENSE OF PEACE AND COMFORT AT HOME.

IN SEARCH OF HARMONY

DESIGNS THAT REJUVENATE

PREVIOUS PAGES: Give a sunny room a golden glow with pale ochre walls that lift the spirits. Burnished wood tables from around the world echo the warm tones in the antique Oriental rugs. To promote lively, yet relaxing conversation, introduce a chaise lounge into your living room seating arrangment.
Photo: www.davidduncanlivingston.com

ABOVE: Muted red walls and soft pillows combine peacefully with natural wood and available light, creating an inviting space to read or relax.
Photo: Peter Margonelli
Design: Benjamin Noriega-Ortiz

OPPOSITE: Create tranquility using natural elements in an entryway. Primitive artwork is visually stimulating and provides a calming, rustic accent to the compact space.
Photo: Coll Photography
Design: Doree Friedman

Understanding harmony is the first step to achieving it. According to the dictionary, harmony is congruity—the combination of parts into an orderly, peaceful whole. We know it best in music where voices join together to turn a simple tune into a spine-tingling choral piece. Simply singing the right notes, however, does not make music. The subtler, intuitive components of loud and soft, sweet and harsh turn the notes into song.

So in our lives, components can coexist—career and home, work and play—but in order for life to be harmonious, there needs to be balance among them. In today's world this is becoming more and more challenging. As we scramble to meet increasing demands, it is ever more difficult to take time for ourselves to rejuvenate body and soul. The more successful we are, the more demands we create for our time and money. The scales begin to tip and life becomes less manageable.

This is where the harmonious home becomes indispensable. A home that welcomes and comforts is restorative. If one can open the front door at the end of the day and instantly feel a sense of calm, the rejuvenation begins even if there is still dinner to make, the dog to walk, laundry to fold, and homework to supervise.

Home does not need to be a showpiece to provide tranquility, but it does need to be composed thoughtfully. Like the melodic soprano voice in a choral piece, a beautiful sofa in a room with compatible fabrics, lighting, pattern, and other forms becomes more lovely as part of its setting. Some element must link furnishings and accessories for a room to be harmonious. The style, color, size, or shape of furnishings and accents should be in accord. This does not mean they should perfectly match, but there must be some thread that ties them together. Choose pieces with some association or connection to contribute to an orderly, tranquil setting. A club chair can work in a delicate, feminine décor if upholstered in a soft color or floral fabric. Or an ornately decorated mirror can work in a casual room if linked by size, color, or material.

Perhaps most important, the décor of a home should be in accord with its inhabitants. As you select furnishings and colors, feel their impact on you. Choose pieces that agree with your own tastes and lifestyle so your home will reflect yourself for a truly harmonious interior.

PAIR A SOLID-COLORED SOFA WITH A CHAIR UPHOLSTERED IN A SUBTLE PRINT THAT CONTAINS THE COLOR OF THE SOFA. ❀ LIFT A COLOR FROM AN ORIENTAL CARPET FOR DRAPERY FABRIC. ❀ USE NATURAL WOOD FURNISHINGS IN A ROOM WITH THE RUSTIC LOOK OF AN EXPOSED BRICK WALL. ❀ AVOID OVERSIZED FURNISHINGS IN A SMALL ROOM. A HUGE SOFA, NO MATTER HOW INVITING, WILL MAKE A TINY TV ROOM FEEL UNCOMFORTABLE. CHOOSE A SUMPTUOUS LOVESEAT INSTEAD FOR THE SAME IMPRESSION WITHOUT THE BULK. ❀ PULL TOGETHER ECLECTIC FURNISHINGS WITH COLOR, OR USE SIMILAR FURNITURE STYLES TO UNITE A ROOM WITH A VARIED PALETTE.

CONGRUITY OF FORM AND FUNCTION ALSO CONTRIBUTES TO A HARMONIOUS INTERIOR. ❀ UPHOLSTER CASUAL FURNISHINGS WITH STURDY FABRICS. ❀ CHOOSE RESTFUL HUES FOR RESTING SPACES. GREENS THAT REJUVENATE, BLUES THAT RELAX, OR UNCOMPLICATED NEUTRALS ARE GOOD CHOICES. ❀ GIVE A HOUSE ON THE BEACH A BREEZY, OPEN-AIR LOOK; LET AN URBAN DWELLING REFLECT THE CHARMS OF THE CITY.

LEFT: Transform your reading corner into a luxurious retreat. To the essential seating, storage, and lighting, add lush upholstery fabric, plump pillows, a cozy cashmere throw, fresh flowers, and candlelight for maximum rejuvenation.
Photo: courtesy of Spiegel

LEFT: Gather richly colored and textured treasures to create a harmonious still life. A collection of Chinese export porcelain and big pillows in a colorful print conjure a warm, casual look while keeping the living room peacefully uncluttered.
Photo: Tony Berardi/Photofields

BELOW LEFT: To create a peaceful space for two, upholster armchairs in soft, muted solid colors and cover bare floors with the neutral, all-over pattern of a coir rug. Feel the cares of the day drain away as you share an intimate cup of tea.
Photo: www.davidduncanlivingston.com

OPPOSITE: Everyone needs a little solitude to recover from the stresses of the day. Set up a corner for yourself with a comfortable chair and surround it with the things you love. Warm earthy tones add a soothing quality to the space.
Photo: www.davidduncanlivingston.com

ABOVE: Hang double drapery over expansive windows
in a large bedroom to generate a sense of security and
shelter while providing versatility for light and view.
Heavy, dark wood furnishings upholstered in neutral
tones anchor the space with their density. The result
is understated elegance in a room that invites repose
by day or night.
Photo: courtesy of Dialogica
Design: Monique and Sergio Savarese

OPPOSITE: Choose earthy tones in a rustic structure
for a comfortable, casual feeling. Shuttered windows
against a painted brick wall provide privacy and a fin-
ished look. Heavy furnishings and distressed wood
invite curling up with the Sunday paper.
Photo: Eric A. Roth
Design: Peter Wheeler

ABOVE: A few well-chosen pieces linked by color and form can complete a room and create a welcoming atmosphere.
Photo: Tony Berardi/ Photofields

OPPOSITE: Turn a confined dining nook into a serene space where you can linger over coffee and dessert. Open-back chairs and a glass-front cabinet make the monochromatic palette feel open and airy.
Photo: Sam Gray Photography
Design: Bierly-Drake

ABOVE: Let a versatile daybed provide stylish seating by day and extra sleeping space for guests at night. It also provides the perfect place for a quick nap after finishing that great novel.
Photo: Tony Berardi/Photofields

RIGHT: Capture the tranquility of nature with a bamboo theme. You can almost hear it rustle in the breeze. Sofa fabric stays neutral so that floor and cushion fabrics add drama to the earth tones.
Photo: www.davidduncanlivingston.com

ABOVE: Use a leaf-patterned motif to evoke instant tranquility in a cozy reading corner.
This fern fabric offers the lift of greenery without detracting from the serenity of the
neutral palette.
Photo: Russell Abraham
Design: Donald Maxcy

OPPOSITE: Set up a reading corner in the bedroom for a private getaway from the activity
of the home. Keep it simple and uncluttered so as not to disturb the sleeping ambience.
A honey colored leather chair and ottoman work well with the creamy tones in this
restful room. The color is picked up in accents on the bedding. Close the door and enjoy a
quiet moment!
Photo: Colin McRae
Design: Jula Sutta

ABOVE: Create the cozy feel of a window seat even without a window. Hang drapery and a valance to delineate the space. A built in seat provides both a peaceful place to read and storage space for books below.
Photo: Steve Vierra
Design: Marian Glasgow

RIGHT: In a large living area create two distinct sitting spaces for a more intimate feel. Here neutral tones link the two while glass tables complement expansive windows and heighten the effect of the cityscape outside.
Photo: Ira Montgomery
Lighting Desing: Barbara Bouyea
Interior Design: Cheri Etchelecu
Architecture: Bill Booziotis/Holly Hall

LEFT: A variety of rich colors and textures give this cozy nook a sense of peace amidst book-lined walls and comfortable furnishings.
Photo: Eric Roth

ABOVE: Get the effect of stucco walls with stippled paint. Simple
furnishings and earthy tones enhance the Old World charm of
terra-cotta tile floors and natural wood shutters.
Photo: Dennis Anderson
Lighting Design, Randall Whitehead and Catherine Ng
Interior Design: Carol Saal
Architecture: Stan Field

OPPOSITE: Use strong, dark colors and adjustable lighting in the living
room to evoke the grandeur of a fine old theater as you watch the night
sky close over the city—a peaceful way to end the day.
Photo: Alan Weintraub
Lighting Design: Becca Foster
Interior Design: Victoria Stone

ABOVE: In a simple structure with plain white walls, furnishings create the style. Mix antiques and modern pieces, add textures and lively colors for a bedroom that chases away the blues.
Photo: Conrad Johnson
Design: Lorcan O'Herlihy

OPPOSITE: Stain exposed wood ceiling and beams in light taupe for a soft, inviting ambience. Light walls and carpet and furnishings accented with warm pastels create a relaxing look and feel.
Photo: Russell Abraham
Design: Ruth Soforenko

LEFT: Turn a plain room into a dramatic setting. Structural pedestals alter the shape of the room and provide display space. In this room, the classic sculptural pieces set a serious tone, carried through with the rich color palette and classic artwork.
Photo: Roland Beaufre
Design: Eric Caspers Ciborowski

HARMONY WITH NATURE

LETTING THE OUTSIDE IN

Our search for harmony stems, in part, from the loss of our connection to nature, a casualty of modern life with both its hectic pace and its focus on physical comfort. The quest for protection from the elements has evolved into almost total insulation from the natural world. As we rush from subway to office, car to shopping mall, we lose sight of our natural surroundings and a sense of connection with a whole. Relieved of our ancestors' struggles to survive, we nonetheless crave the soothing effects of nature. Do we know the smell of a spring rain anymore, the stillness before a storm? We view nature as an occasional element in our lives as we travel miles to experience the wonder of an ocean breeze or a mountain stream.

But nature is all around us. With a little attention, we can reincorporate it into our lives. Even in the city, birds sing in the trees and spiders spin their webs. Notice how the light changes with the seasons, how the wind sounds in the night, how rain patters against your windows. Feel the sensations these natural events evoke. They can supplant the agitation of daily life with a sense of harmony and well-being.

Infuse your home with a sense of calm by incorporating the world outside into your décor. Although more easily accomplished in less-populated areas than in an urban setting, even a glimpse of sky or a single tree at the window can be enough to recall the feeling of a walk in the woods or the vastness of the desert sky. Choose colors and materials that augment the environment surrounding your home. Play up the view you have or introduce elements into your home that provide their own subtle link to nature.

Get the most from your surroundings and luxuriate in their soothing effect. A home will feel especially welcoming if the interior reflects its natural setting. Work within the style and setting of your home, in a mode that suits your taste, for a harmonious home from the outside in.

PREVIOUS PAGES: Merge landscaping and interior décor. Match interior colors to plantings outside and include container plants inside. You will feel as though you are sleeping under the stars.
Photo: Grey Crawford
Design: Lorcan O'Herlihy

ABOVE: Give dark wood furnishings a light touch with gauzy fabrics and a subdued palette and let the beachfront view provide the vibrancy.
Photo: www.davidduncanlivingston.com

OPPOSITE: Revel in the luxury of a three-season porch. Sink into an upholstered chair and feel nature soothe your weary spirit.
Photo: www.davidduncanlivingston.com

USE BREEZY COLORS AND AIRY FABRICS TO EMPHASIZE THE OPEN-AIR FEELING OF A BEACHFRONT HOME. ❀ CAPTURE THE ATMOSPHERE OF A MOUNTAIN LODGE WITH EARTHY COLORS AND BOLD PRINTS ON RUSTIC FURNISHINGS. ❀ ECHO THE MAGIC OF A WOODLAND SETTING WITH LEAFY TONES IN YOUR PALETTE. ❀ ORIENT FURNISHINGS TOWARD WINDOWS FOR WATCHING THE SUNSET. ❀ AVOID WINDOW TREATMENTS ALTOGETHER AND CUE YOUR COLOR PALETTE TO THE WORLD OUTSIDE YOUR WINDOWS.

❀ TURN A ROOFTOP INTO A COUNTRY GARDEN WHERE YOU CAN IGNORE THE BUSTLE OF THE STREET BELOW. OR MAKE THE MOST OF A SMALL PATCH OF LAWN OR YARD JUST OUTSIDE YOUR DOOR. ❀ SURROUND COMFORTABLE SEATING AREAS WITH AN ABUNDANCE OF POTTED PLANTS. ❀ USE FLEA MARKET FINDS FOR A WEATHERED, RUSTIC LOOK. ❀ LET THE SOFT GLOW OF LANTERNS ILLUMINATE A SPACE FOR EVENING USE. ❀ SET AN OUTDOOR TABLE WITH CANDLELIGHT AND FLOWERS FOR A ROMANTIC DINNER FOR TWO ALFRESCO.

❀ A THREE-SEASON PORCH CAPTURES THE PLEASURES OF THE OUTDOORS WHILE PROVIDING WARMTH AND SHELTER. OUTFIT IT FOR MAXIMAL USE WITHIN YOUR LIFESTYLE. ❀ USE FABRICS AND PATTERNS TO ENHANCE THE OUTDOOR FEEL. ❀ INCLUDE A TABLE AND CHAIRS FOR CASUAL DINING. ❀ ADD A COMFORTABLE CHAIR FOR AN AFTERNOON READ. ❀ FURNISH THE PORCH WITH A GAME TABLE FOR FAMILY ENJOYMENT. ❀ PROVIDE GOOD LIGHTING SO THIS INDOOR/OUTDOOR SPACE CAN WORK ITS MAGIC EVEN ON RAINY DAYS.

LEFT: Extend your bedroom to the outside through atrium doors. A cool palette and a cozy Oriental for bare feet makes one eager to greet a summer day.
Photo: Coll Photography
Design: Doree Friedman

OPPOSITE: With an expanse of green lawn for a backdrop, a three-season porch feels like part of the outdoors. Allow the natural wood to mingle with the setting for maximum effect.
Photo: courtesy of Exposures

RIGHT ABOVE AND BELOW: Create your own forest with an atrium off your den. Fill the windows with the greenery of tall, potted plants and let your mind take you to a cottage in the woods.
Photo: Marianne Haas
Design: Francois Catroux

ABOVE: Turn a balcony into a treetop garden. The birds and flowers will love it as much as you do.
Photo: Mark Lohman
Design: Sandy Koepke

OPPOSITE: Furnish your covered porch with coir and wicker and a profusion of potted plants. What better place to sip iced tea on a warm afternoon?
Photo: Mark Lohman
Design: Larry and Kathy Keele

ABOVE: Set up a comfortable corner in your country kitchen for enjoying the morning paper in a warm patch of sunlight.
Photo: Eric Roth

LEFT: Slide a translucent shoji screen open for exotic indoor/outdoor living. You can almost smell the cherry blossoms.
Photo: Tony Berardi/Photofields

ABOVE: Even in a city apartment with small windows, let the outside in. Use bright wall hang-
ings and leave the windows bare to draw the eye to passing clouds and the stars by night.
Photo: Tony Beradi/Photofields

OPPOSITE: Complement hardwood floors with wicker and an airy neutral palette for a
barefoot-in-summer feel all year long.
Photo: courtesy of Nono

ABOVE: Try channeled translucent glass for an impressionistic aura of shimmering greenery and light.
Photo: Tom Bonner
Design: Lorcan O'Herlihy

LEFT: Use natural materials in the kitchen and feel your home nestle into the surrounding woods.
Photo: Richard Barnes
Design: Fu.Tung Cheng

ABOVE LEFT: Immerse yourself in your ocean view. Minimalist furnishings and bare windows make you feel like you live on the beach.
Photo: Tom Bonner
Design: Lorcan O'Herlihy

LEFT: Bask in the sunlight without leaving the comfort of your home. Bare windows and a sand-white interior mimic a glistening poolside patio.
Photo: Jeremy Samuelson
Design: Lorcan O'Herlihy

BELOW: Link patio and living room with terra-cotta flooring and container plants on both. You will hardly know if you are inside or out.
Photo: Conrad Johnson
Design: Lorcan O'Herlihy

OPPOSITE: A pair of cushioned chaises turns a protected porch into a perfect place for watching the sunset with your mate or dozing on a sultry afternoon.
Photo: courtesy of Spiegel

ABOVE: Filter sunlight through slatted wooden blinds for a cool plantation feel in a summer bedroom. A cotton runner subtly extends the room to the porch outside.
Photo: Timothy Hursley, courtesy of *House Beautiful*
Design: Lake/Flato

LEFT: Watch the sunset from a rooftop hideaway. Add a kilim and lots of pillows for a romantic evening under the stars.
Photo: David Glomb
Design: Brad Blair

ABOVE: Furnish a breezeway for casual meals in the spirit of summer.
Photo: Mark Darley, courtesy of *House Beautiful*
Design: William Turnbull

OPPOSITE: Take full advantage of your piece of the outdoors. Set up a fresh-air bathing spot with just enough shelter to feel private and enough fluffy towels to feel luxurious.
Photo: Mark Darley, courtesy of *House Beautiful*
Design: William Turnbull

LEFT, ABOVE, AND FOLLOWING PAGES: Create a landscape to rival any rural outdoor spot with a profusion of flowering plants in a garden arrangement on stepped decks that mimic nature's irregularities. A cabaña-style tool shed adds an exotic touch and provides shelter for tools and children's tricycles.
Photos: Kari Haavisto, courtesy of *House Beautiful*
Design: Walter Chatham

ABOVE: Turn your city rooftop into an outdoor retreat.
Surrounded by greenery and blue sky, you will forget the
traffic and bustle below.
Photo: Kari Haavisto, courtesy of *House Beautiful*
Design: Walter Chatham

OPPOSITE: Convert a city rooftop into a country estate
with potted herbs and flowers against a brick backdrop
for an open-air dining room.
Photo: Scott Frances, courtesy of *House Beautiful*
Design: Walter Chatham

HARMONY THROUGHOUT THE HOME

ROOMS THAT WORK IN CONCERT

PREVIOUS PAGES: Suspend light drapery in an
archway between two rooms. A monochromatic
color scheme unites the two while the drapery
defines their limits and creates a breezy
resting place.
Photo: Peter Margonelli
Design: Benjamin Noriega-Ortiz

LEFT: Choose a color you love and use it in varying
intensities throughout your home. Deep rosy
pink and petal pink work together to create a
vivacious yet gentle look; one excites the space as
the other softens it.
Photo: Brady Architectual Photography
Design: Laura Birns

OPPOSITE: Cherry red is even livelier against
apple green in an adjacent room. The complementary colors enhance each other, giving the
whole space a cheerful glow.
Photo: Grey Crawford
Design: Jeffrey Alan Marks

Our homes are a reflection of our lives. We blend various aspects of our lives into a harmonious whole, but if there is tension between one component and another we feel the resulting stress. So in our homes, separate areas must work well together. The comfort each provides is dependent upon the others.

In a traditional home, rooms are separate but not isolated from one another. Create harmony among them as well as within them. Give the various rooms some association, making a graceful transition from one to another.

There is an inherent flow to homes with open floor plans. Reap the benefits of the expansiveness and minimize the drawbacks by visually linking separate areas of activity while at the same time maintaining the integrity of each. The spaces should work as well separately as they do together; that is, the activity in one should not detract from the others. For instance, the benefit of visiting with family or guests as you work unimpeded in the kitchen could be outweighed by the discomfort of having to look at the clutter of meal preparation while eating dinner.

Outfit each area so that it functions well on its own: Let your sitting area invite repose, the dining area entice diners to linger over coffee and dessert, and the kitchen function efficiently and fade as a work-space when not in use. At the same time, take in the whole sweep of space as you make decorating choices. Harmony will pervade the entire home if the various areas are compatible.

Whether your home is several rooms or just one, aim for accord, not uniformity. Play with accents in each area. Bounce colors back and forth between them. Tie them together with repetition of form, how-ever subtle, and they will blend into a harmonious whole.

WALL COLOR CAN DRAW ROOMS TOGETHER. ✤ PAINT WALLS A NEUTRAL TONE AND VARY ACCENTS FROM ROOM TO ROOM TO GIVE THEM EACH DISTINCT APPEAL. ✤ CHOOSE CLOSELY RELATED COLORS OF THE SAME VALUE FOR ADJACENT ROOMS. FOR EXAMPLE, MUTED BLUE-GREEN WILL WORK WELL WITH A SIMILARLY-MUTED YELLOW-GREEN NEARBY. ✤ USE COMPLEMENTARY COLORS IN ADJACENT ROOMS AND ACCENT EACH WITH THE PREDOMINANT COLOR OF THE OTHER: PALE BLUE WALLS WITH PEACH ACCENTS IN ONE ROOM; PEACH WALLS WITH LIGHT BLUE ACCENTS IN THE ADJACENT ROOM. ✤ CHOOSE ONE COLOR AND VARY ITS INTENSITY FROM ROOM TO ROOM.

OR LET FURNISHINGS BE THE LINK BETWEEN AREAS OF THE HOME. ✤ A DARK, HEAVY TABLE AND EARTHENWARE DISPLAYED IN THE DINING ROOM WILL COMPLEMENT A CASUAL LIVING ROOM WITH COMFORTABLE FURNITURE IN NATURAL FABRICS. ✤ GIVE DIFFERENT ROOMS A SIMILAR FEEL WITH SLEEK CONTEMPORARY FURNITURE AND STYLISTIC ARTWORK ON THE WALLS. ✤ USE FLORAL ACCENTS OF A SIMILAR PATTERN FOR PILLOWS, THROWS, DRAPERIES, OR LAMPSHADES TO LINK ROOMS. ✤ MATCH THE COLOR OF THE LIVING ROOM SOFA TO THE SEAT COVERS OF THE DINING ROOM CHAIRS. ✤ ORIENTAL CARPETS IN EACH ROOM CAN VARY IN COLOR AND PATTERN WHILE CREATING AN ASSOCIATION BETWEEN THE ROOMS.

✤ ADORN KITCHEN WALLS WITH ARTWORK TO COMPLEMENT THE DINING AREA. ✤ MATCH CUSTOM KITCHEN CABINETS TO A BUILT-IN BUFFET IN THE DINING ROOM TO TIE THE TWO SPACES TOGETHER. ✤ STASH SMALL APPLIANCES BEHIND SLIDING DOORS ON THE KITCHEN COUNTER. WHEN NOT IN USE, THE KITCHEN WILL LOOK LESS LIKE A WORKSPACE IF TOOLS ARE HIDDEN. ✤ IF YOUR HOME HAS AN OPEN KITCHEN-LIVING ROOM LAYOUT, CONCEAL DIRTY POTS AND PANS FROM THE DINING AREA. ✤ PAIR THE CLEAN, SPARE LINES OF FLAT-FRONT CABINETS IN THE KITCHEN WITH LOW, SLEEK LIVING ROOM FURNITURE. ✤ IN THE LIVING AREA, CHOOSE LOW-BACKED SEATING IF IT WILL BE PLACED AWAY FROM THE WALL. TALLER SOFAS AND CHAIRS INTERRUPT THE SWEEPING EXPANSE OF SPACE.

LEFT: Infuse serenity into an active, open floor plan with clean lines and quiet colors. House your audio and video equipment in a built-in unit that matches sleek kitchen cabinets, a restful backdrop for melding family activity and meal preparation.
Photo: Richard Barnes
Design: Fu Tung Cheng

ABOVE: A glimpse of serene dining space with ochre walls and Eastern accessories warms the pristine white of an adjoining room. Against the white, the dining area becomes almost jewel-like.
Photo: Tim Street-Porter
Design: Thomas M. Beeton

OPPOSITE: Accentuate an archway with dramatic lighting. The room beyond becomes a framed picture in sympathetic tones.
Photo: Coll Photography
Design: Doree Friedman

ABOVE: Create a dreamy space for luxuriating in summer's splendor. Diaphanous silk drapery and an icy blue palette imbue these rooms with the freshness of an ocean breeze.
Photo: Peter Margonelli
Design: Benjamin Noriega-Ortiz

RIGHT: Complementary pastel hues are a good choice for a cluster of bedrooms. Their lovely, soft tones work together to enhance the peacefulness of the entire area.
Photo: Eric A. Roth

LEFT: Kitchen cabinets that match dining room walls help the open workspace recede into the background when not in use. Add a touch of elegance with a gleaming range hood.
Photo: Steve Vierra

ABOVE: Make the rooms in your home variations on a common style. A Native American blanket and a brightly colored door make a southwestern statement as do aged plaster walls and the mission cross of the same bright color in the adjoining room. The distinctive look of each room enhances that of the other, creating a richer whole.
Photo: Tim Street-Porter

ABOVE: Make the most of open space in a natural setting. Use coir rugs to delineate areas
and wicker furnishings paired with rugged cotton for a relaxed, fresh air feeling.
Photo: Mikio Sekita
Design: Davis + Maltz Architects

OPPOSITE: In an open floor plan, link distinct areas with color. Echo the peach tones
from the living room upholstery in the dining room chairs, giving the entire space a lively,
inviting look.
Photo: Eric A. Zepeda
Interior Design: Priscilla Sanchez
Architecture: George Sinclair

LEFT: Choose an unconventional color for moldings and trim to lead the eye from room to room, uniting separate spaces with a restful "frame."
Photo: Coll Photography
Design: Doree Friedman

ABOVE: Match your kitchen cabinetry to warm cherry paneling in the dining room. When the door is ajar, the kitchen becomes an extension of the glowing dining ambience.
Photo: Grey Crawford
Design: William Hefner

ABOVE: Set off the weight of a dark wood ceiling with bright white walls. Choose Oriental rugs and rich, dark furnishings for a dignified, yet unconstrained look.
Photo: Bill Rothschild

RIGHT: Give your whole home a cohesive, stately feel. A sedate neutral palette gives stature to fine furnishings throughout.
Photo: Philip Harvey
Lighting Design: Linda Ferry
Architecture: Lee von Hasseln

ABOVE: Use a creamy palette for presentation of black and white art
in a softened atmosphere more restful than stark white.
Photo: William Mackenzie-Smith
Design: Alisa Smith

OPPOSITE: Display sculpture in gallery fashion to give distinct rooms
a similarity of form that eases the transition from one to the other.
Photo: John Sutton
Design: Gary Hutton

THE HOME OFFICE

BALANCING WORK AND HOME

More of us are finding ways to work at home in order to ease tension in our multifaceted lives, balancing the need to work with both the responsibilities and the pleasures of home and family. But actually achieving this equilibrium can be quite a challenge. Trying to close a business deal over the clamor of kids while dinner burns on the stove is not an improvement. If your family demands are great, quiet work time can be scarce. If you live alone, work can expand to fill all your time. The solution is to keep work and household tasks separate, while reaping the benefit of melding the two. Enjoy the relief from the stressful commute, the freedom to schedule work to accommodate home demands, and the tranquility of working in a home setting, while being mindful not to infuse each with the stresses of the other.

Separate work time and home time so that you are not constantly juggling both. How you manage this depends upon your work and family demands, but now you have the flexibility to tailor the day to accommodate your needs. It can help to set a schedule with uninterrupted time for each. Do not let household chores encroach on your work time, and vice versa. Allow time to concentrate when working, time to take care of household tasks, and time to put up your feet and relax.

A distinct space to work is also essential. Set up an area to suit your specific requirements with ample work surfaces, storage, and task lighting, and segregate it from other activities. If you cannot completely isolate your office, hide your desk when not in use with a folding screen or drapery, or provide a drawer to stash your current project at the end of the day, leaving uncluttered surfaces for family time. It is hard to forget about work if it is right in front of you.

Comfort is as important as efficiency. Pay attention to ergonomics, especially if you work at a computer for long stretches. Proper monitor height, keyboard position, and seating will protect against injury. Without the distractions of others in a busy office, you risk staying in one position too long. Allow yourself to take breaks. Stand up and stretch, wiggle your fingers, and rotate your wrists.

Make your office a pleasant room, keep it uncluttered, and it will be a comfortable, tranquil place in which to create a masterpiece, meet those deadlines, or negotiate those deals. At the end of the day, tidy up your desk, turn out the light, walk out and close the door behind you. Home at last!

NCLUDE DECORATIVE ELEMENTS FOR PLEASURE ALONE—A PAINTING THAT DRAWS YOU IN, A FAVORITE FABRIC AS A WALL HANGING OR CURTAINS, FRESH FLOWERS OR POTTED PLANTS. ✾ ORIENT YOUR DESK SO YOU CATCH A GLIMPSE OF THE OUTSIDE. ✾ INCLUDE A RADIO OR CD PLAYER FOR THE SOOTHING EFFECTS OF MUSIC AS YOU WORK. ✾ INSTALL A MINI REFRIGERATOR TO KEEP ENERGY-BOOSTING SNACKS NEARBY AND BOTTLED WATER HANDY TO HELP REACH THAT BARELY ATTAINABLE 8-GLASSES-A-DAY GOAL.

REGARDLESS OF HOW MUCH TIME YOU SPEND IN YOUR HOME OFFICE, MAKE IT A SPACE YOU ENJOY. ✾ IF YOU HAVE SALVAGED FURNITURE FROM THE ATTIC, GIVE IT A FACELIFT FOR ITS NEW LIFE. ✾ PAINT WOODEN FURNISHINGS AND MASK TATTERED UPHOLSTERY WITH A LIVELY TABLECLOTH OR SHEET IN A PATTERN THAT FITS THE DÉCOR. OR, IF YOU CAN, INVEST IN FURNISHINGS TO SUIT YOUR TASTE. DO NOT BUY FOR EFFICIENCY ALONE. ✾ MODULAR UNITS ARE AVAILABLE IN A WIDE VARIETY OF STYLES AND CONFIGURATIONS, OR GO FOR A FREESTANDING, FINELY CRAFTED DESK AND A LEATHER EXECUTIVE CHAIR. FOR PROLONGED READING, ADD AN UPHOLSTERED CHAIR AND OTTOMAN WITH A GOOD READING LAMP.

✾ CHOOSE COLORS YOU LOVE THAT WILL ENHANCE YOUR WORK. RESTFUL BLUES, GREENS, OR NEUTRALS PROVIDE A PEACEFUL BACKDROP FOR CREATIVE THINKING. OR GIVE YOURSELF THE ENERGIZING BOOST OF STIMULATING REDS AND YELLOWS FOR ANIMATED SALES CALLS. ✾ KEEP A COZY THROW NEARBY FOR CHILLY DAYS.✾ PROVIDE AMBIENT LIGHTING TO BRIGHTEN THE WHOLE SPACE. THERE IS NOTHING DREARIER THAN BEING ALONE IN A DARK OFFICE ON A RAINY DAY. GIVE YOURSELF THE LUXURY OF WORKING IN A HARMONIOUS SPACE AND FEEL YOUR PRODUCTIVITY IMPROVE.

Create an inspirational workspace with a large, marble-topped table as a luxurious writing space. Floor-to-ceiling bookshelves on one wall provide plenty of storage, while classical columns and friezes on another set the tone for scholarly endeavors.
Photo: Guillaume de Laubier
Design: Didier Gomez

ABOVE: With the abundance of workstations available, you can set up an efficient office in just a corner. But put work out of sight at the end of the day so it will not encroach on home time.
Photo: Ken Rice

LEFT: Keep the work flowing while simultaneously alleviating stress with mauve walls that blend the energizing effects of red with the relaxing quality of blue. Draw the drapes at the end of the day and forget about work until tomorrow!
Photo: Ken Rice

A lush, velvet sleeper sofa lets your office double as a guest room and provides a perfect
spot for stretching out while you go over those reports.
Photo: Eric Roth

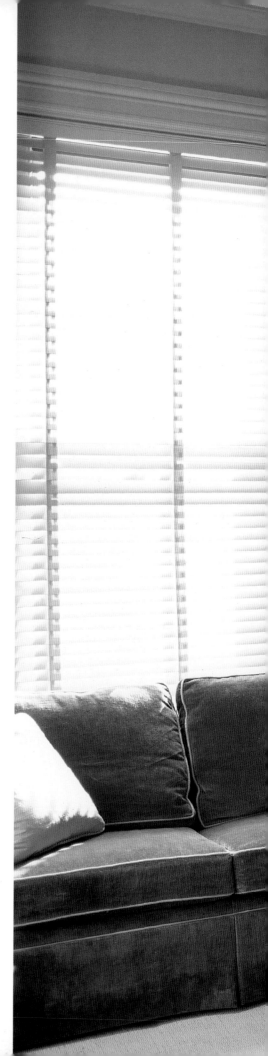

ABOVE: Use a modular system for plenty of storage space and sweeping work surfaces.
Choose a light, restful tone to balance stimulating deep-red walls.
Photo: Ken Rice

OPPOSITE: Enjoy working in the sunlight, but avoid a distracting view with translucent
screens shielding the windows. Create an interior landscape instead with plants and
a cactus-like sculpture.
Photo:© Bill Geddes, 1999
Design: Dakota Jackson

Transform a basement laundry area [above] into a bright, energizing workspace [left]. Small doses of primary colors work their magic—sparking creativity while livening white space.
Photos: Ken Rice

RIGHT: Think about your specific needs as
you design your space. Perhaps counter-
height surfaces will serve you better
than a desk.
Photo: Ken Rice

ABOVE AND RIGHT: Include storage for unwieldy plans and large-format layouts to help
keep your space tidy and manageable.
Photos: Ken Rice

LEFT: Transform a bedroom closet into
bookshelves and plenty of storage to
conceal the disarray of files and supplies.
Photo: Ken Rice

ABOVE: Keep an uncluttered look with cabinets instead of open shelving. All manner of supplies and projects can be kept behind the doors without disturbing the clear work space.
Photo: Ken Rice

RIGHT: Orient your desk to take advantage of a tree-lined view. A glimpse of the natural world has an exhilarating effect as you puzzle over a sticky problem.
Photo: Ken Rice

LEFT: Work in a warm glow with golden walls that give life to an enclosed office space. Use dark accents and varied textures for an aura that suggests established success.
Photo: Brady Architectural Photography
Design: Linda Medina and Marylin Matson

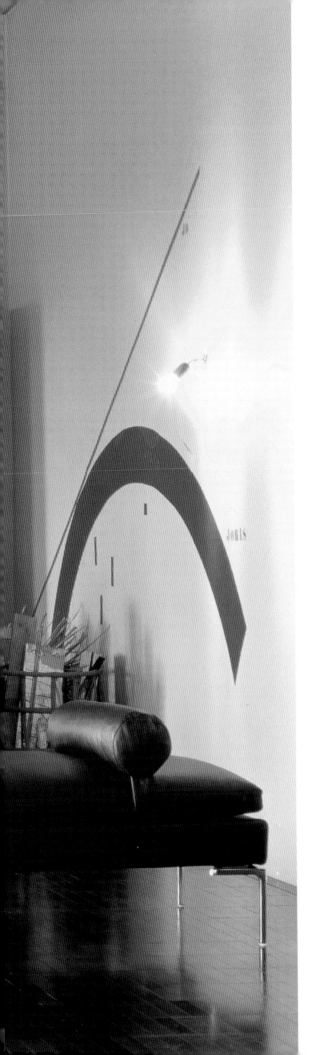

FENG SHUI

ANCIENT REMEDIES TO BALANCE YOUR LIFE

The desire for harmony in our homes and in our lives is not a new
phenomenon. For centuries the Chinese have called upon practitioners of feng shui, the art of placement, for guidance in achieving this
goal. Literally translated as "wind and water," feng shui was originally
developed to locate burial sites attuned to the natural forces, but its
practice expanded to include auspicious positioning of buildings and
possessions.

Feng shui is a rich discipline with broad roots in ancient philosophies
and religions, superstition, and magic. Practitioners study under
masters for years to gain the knowledge and insight necessary to
become experts in the field. But while feng shui is quite complicated
and even mysterious, its basic tenet is simple and intuitive: we are
affected by our surroundings. A harmonious home, then, will aid in
the pursuit of a harmonious life.

Concepts such as Tao, yin and yang, and ch'i inform this belief. The
doctrine of **Tao, "the way,"** is that all things are interconnected.
Taoists seek a way in the world that will not cause disruption to
cosmic forces. Feng shui guides the positioning of our homes and
belongings within the home to accommodate and benefit from the
natural order, rather than intruding upon it. ✹ Choose a building site
on the south side of a hill or mountain rather than the north. This
affords protection from the elements and optimizes available light.
✹ Inside the home, position major furnishings—beds, kitchen stove,
desk, sofa—so that someone using them can see the entryway,
relieving them of the unsettling feeling of not knowing what is
happening behind them. Where this is not possible, hang a mirror or
reflective object to keep doors in the line of sight.

The concept of **yin and yang** is that a balanced whole is attained only through inclusion of opposites. A home with "good" feng shui includes balanced representations of female and male, light and dark, soft and hard, curvilinear and straight. ❀ Balance the yang of angular furnishings with a round cocktail table to introduce yin. ❀ Offset dark wood furnishings and carpet (yang) with bright daylight from a large window or light-colored walls (yin).

Ch'i is positive natural energy. Its flow through a place affects the inhabitants. Feng shui provides cures to excite or slow down ch'i as needed for it to flow freely, but not so quickly that it passes through without effect. Areas of the home are linked to specific aspects of our lives, determined by their relative positions. Enhancing the flow of ch'i in the Relationships area, for example, is believed to aid in finding a mate or in strengthening an existing relationship.

The **bagua** (see figure opposite) is the tool used to determine the locations of the areas of your home that affect your Career, Knowledge, Family, Wealth, Recognition, Relationships, Creativity, Benefactors, and Health, as well as their corresponding colors. Superimpose the bagua centered over a plan of your house, or of a room in your home, with the Career section at the wall of the main entrance. Each area of your home has a designated attribute from the perspective of the home and from the perspective of the room. Thus identified, areas can be treated with feng shui remedies to help attain certain goals.

Try feng shui cures to improve balance in your home, which will in turn improve balance in your life. For a fuller understanding of this practice and guidance in its intricacies, further study is recommended. See **FENG SHUI RESOURCES** on page 139 for a list of books and websites.

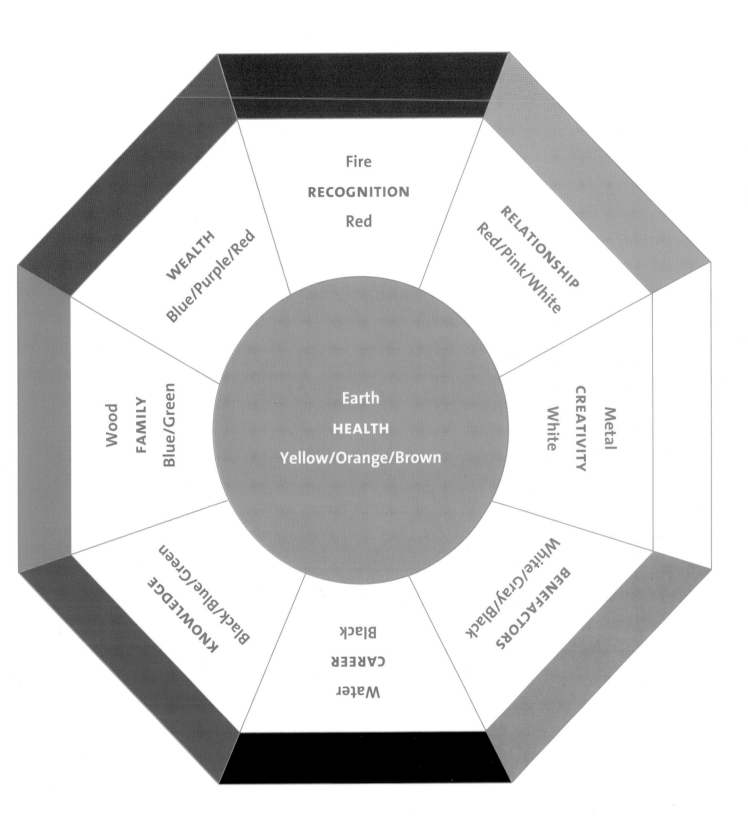

Fire
RECOGNITION
Red

RELATIONSHIP
Red/Pink/White

WEALTH
Blue/Purple/Red

FAMILY
Wood
Blue/Green

Earth
HEALTH
Yellow/Orange/Brown

Metal
CREATIVITY
White

KNOWLEDGE
Black/Blue/Green

Water
CAREER
Black

BENEFACTORS
White/Gray/Black

THE FIVE BASIC ELEMENTS—EARTH, WATER, WOOD, FIRE, AND METAL—ARE ALSO DISPLAYED ON THE BAGUA. IT IS BELIEVED THAT REAL OR REPRESENTATIONAL INCLUSION OF THESE ELEMENTS EXCITES POSITIVE CH'I AND ENHANCES THAT ASPECT OF YOUR LIFE. FOR EXAMPLE, INCLUDE WOOD IN THE FAMILY AREA TO PROMOTE HARMONY AMONG FAMILY MEMBERS.

ASIDE FROM THE SPECIFIC ATTRIBUTES ADDRESSED BY THE BAGUA, THE PRACTICE OF FENG SHUI INCLUDES FUNDAMENTALS FOR ESTABLISHING BALANCE AND HARMONY IN THE HOME AND, BY EXTENSION, ITS INHABITANTS. ❀ SLOW DOWN CH'I IN YOUR WALKWAY AND ENTRY. A WINDING PATH ENCOURAGES A GENTLER, MORE MEANDERING PACE THAN A STRAIGHT LINE IN FROM THE STREET. IF YOUR HALLWAY IS LONG AND NARROW, MODERATE THE RUSH OF CH'I WITH HANGING CHIMES, A COLORFUL RUNNER, OR ARTWORK ON THE WALLS. ❀ BATHROOM PLUMBING CAN DRAIN CH'I FROM THE HOME AND ITS INHABITANTS. FIX LEAKY FAUCETS AND KEEP THE TOILET LID DOWN. ❀ EXPOSED BEAMS EXERT DOWNWARD PRESSURE. ALLEVIATE THEIR NEGATIVE THRUST WITH HANGING CRYSTALS. ❀ AVOID DISORDER, WHICH INHIBITS THE FREE FLOW OF CH'I. PROVIDE DRAWERS, MAGAZINE RACKS, AND SHELVING TO KEEP CLUTTER FROM ACCUMULATING.

LEFT: Use red, the color of Fire, in the Fame and Recognition area of your home to stimulate ch'i and enhance this aspect of your life.
Photo: www.davidduncanlivingston.com

ABOVE: Let a stainless steel backsplash act as a mirror to prevent a visitor from startling the cook. Stone surfaces add the element of Earth to balance the Wood, Metal, Water, and Fire already found in this kitchen.
Photo: Richard Barnes
Design: Fu Tung Cheng

LEFT: In the bathroom, balance the energy-draining effect of the plumbing with plants representing Wood energy. Draping the toilet in red, the color of Fire, helps to stem the loss of ch'i as well.
Photo: Steve Vierra
Design: Kathleen Fox

ABOVE: Balance yin and yang with a chic black and yellow palette. Try creating a wainscoting effect with wallpaper in a dark color (yang) to contrast the light (yin). The border that links the two here further enhances balance with its curved yin lines offsetting the rectangular yang design of the two papers.
Photo: courtesy of Nono

RIGHT: Wood balances Water and Fire, the two principal elements in the kitchen. Paint your kitchen a tranquil green, the color of Wood, to promote nourishment and support cooking activities.
Photo: Jeff McNamara
Design: Austin Patterson Disston

OPPOSITE: Position your bed so that you can feel safe and relaxed. You should be able to see the doorway without directly facing it, to be able to see if someone enters while avoiding the direct flow of *ch'i*. A dividing wall in a large master bedroom provides a protected niche for the bed. To keep the entry visible, hang a mirror on the wall opposite the door.

Photo: Luis Ferreira Alves
Design: Eduardo Souto Moura

ABOVE: Create an elegant bathing space in an awkward corner with a large tub surround to fill the space. Accessories and plants placed at the foot of the tub soften the "knife edge" of the roofline and reduce the ch'i-draining effect of the plumbing.
Photo: Eric A Roth

OPPOSITE: A vase of fresh flowers can provide the missing colors for a balanced representation of the elements. Yellow and green leaves add Earth and Wood without detracting from the fresh palette of this kitchen.
Photo: Brady Architectural Photography
Design: Laura Birns, ASID

ABOVE: Improve your chances for the spotlight with Fire in the Recognition area.
A section of bright red wall excites Fire ch'i and creates a lively space for quick meals.
Photo: courtesy of Becker Zeyko

OPPOSITE: Oval mirrors reduce the "knife edge" of sharp glass corners. This ornately
framed mirror dazzles while it excites ch'i.
Photo: Mary E. Nichols
Design: Charlotte Jensen, ASID

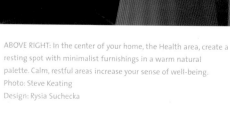

ABOVE: Blue and green will enhance the Family section of your home. Even a small representation of these colors in a collection of decorative glassware represents Wood, tranquility, hope and freshness.
Photo: Ed Gohlich
Design: Maryclare Brandt, ASID

ABOVE RIGHT: In the center of your home, the Health area, create a resting spot with minimalist furnishings in a warm natural palette. Calm, restful areas increase your sense of well-being.
Photo: Steve Keating
Design: Rysia Suchecka

ABOVE LEFT: Excite ch'i in the Recognition area of the living room with a pair of lively red leather chairs, evoking the element of Fire.
Photo: Erhard Pfeiffer
Design: Kanner Architects

ABOVE: Pink, the color that enhances Relationships, is the best color to use in the bedroom. If a pink room does not suit your taste, incorporate a small dose into a look that is right for you. A duvet cover and shams in a classic print will do the trick.
Photo: Steve Vierra
Design: Nancy Reynolds

RIGHT: Choose a glass coffee table with a rounded shape to soften the effects of the edges. The curves (yin) balance the angularity (yang) of the other furnishings.
Photo: Tom Bonner
Design: Lorcan O'Herlihy

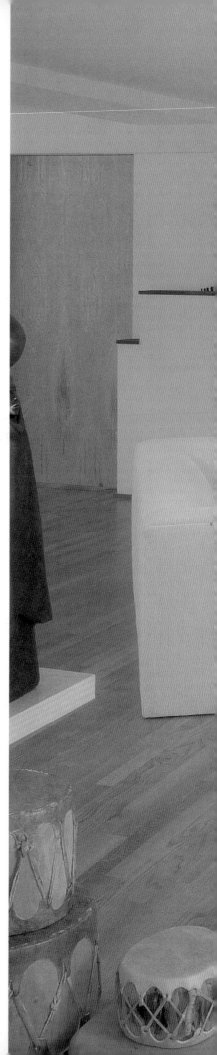

FENG SHUI RESOURCES

BOOKS

Chin, R. D., *Feng Shui Revealed.* New York: Clarkson N. Potter, Inc., member of Crown Publishing Group, 1998.

King, Carol Soucek, *Feng Shui at Home.* New York: PBC International, Inc. ,1999.

Kingston, Karen, *Clear Your Clutter with Feng Shui.* First US edition, New York: Broadway Books, a division of Random House, 1999.

Lazenby, Gina, *The Feng Shui House Book: Change your Home, Transform your Life.* New York: Watson Guptill Publications, a division of BPI Communications, 1998.

Rossbach, Sarah, *Feng Shui: The Chinese Art of Placement.* New York: E. P. Dutton, Inc., 1983.

Rossbach, Sarah and Yun, Lin, *Living Color: Master Lin Yun's Guide to Feng Shui and the Art of Color.* New York: Kodansha America, Inc., 1994.

SantoPietro, Nancy, *Feng Shui: Harmony by Design.* New York: A Perigee Book, The Berkley Publishing Group, a member of Penguin Putnam, Inc., 1996.

Wydra, Nancilee, *Designing Your Happiness: A Contemporary Look at Feng Shui.* Torrance, CA: Heian International, Inc., 1995.

WEB SITES

www.9starki.com
www.fengshui-magazine.com
www.FengShuiLiving.com
www.fengshuisociety.org.uk
www.fengshuiwarehouse.com
www.fsdirectory.com
www.geomany.net
www.qi-whiz.com
www.worldoffengshui.com

DIRECTORY OF DESIGNERS

Marcey Balk
44 West 76th Street #1
New York, NY 10023

Bast/Wright Interiors
307 Eighth Ave.
San Diego, CA 92101

Thomas M. Beeton, Inc.
7231/2 N. La Cienega Blvd.
Los Angeles, CA 90069
Tel: 310-657-5600

Bierly & Drake Assoc.
17 Arlington Street
Boston, MA 02116

Laura Birns, ASID
P.O. Box 812
Del Mar, CA 92014

Brad Blair
Lotis Antiquities
158 N. Le Brea Ave.
Los Angeles, CA 90036
Tel: 323-938-4531

Barbara Bouyea, IALD, IES
Bouyea & Associates
3811 Turtle Creek Blvd, Suite 1010
Dallas, TX 75219
Tel: 241-520-6580
Fax: 241-520-6581

MaryClare Brandt, ASID
MC Brandt Interior Design
P.O. Box 8276
La Jolla, CA 92083

Alberto Campo Baeza
Archetectecto
Almirante, 9
28004 Madrid
Spain
Tel: 34-1-521-7061

Francious Carroux
20 Ru du Faubourg Saint Honore
Paris 75008
France

Eric Caspers Ciborowski
85 bis, rue Billancourt
Boulonge 92000
France

Walter Chatham Architect
580 Broadway
New York, NY 10012
Tel: 212-925-2202
Fax: 212-966-2857

Davis & Maltz Architects
270 Lafeyette St., Suite 307
New York, NY 10012

FSC Wallcoverings
Victoria Pace
79 Madison Ave.
New York, NY 10016
Tel: 212-213-7795
Fax: 212-213-7640

Linda Ferry, IES, ASID
Archectural Illumination
P.O. Box 2690
Monterey, CA 93942
Tel: 408-649-3711
Fax: 408-375-5897

Becca Foster Lighting Design
27 South Park
San Francisco, CA 94107
Tel: 415-541-0370
Fax: 415-957-5856

Doree Friedman
Fineline Construction
1615 Cortland Street
San Francisco, CA 94110

Didier Gomez
Ory Gomez
15 Rue Henri Heine
Paris 75016
France

Gramercy
79 Madison Ave.
New York, NY 10016
Tel: 212- 213- 7795
Fax: 212-213-7640

Jane Page Grump ASID, IIDA
Jane Page Creative Designs Inc.
200 Wescott St.
Houston, TX 77007
Tel: 713-803-4999
Fax: 713-803-4998

William Hefner
5820 Wilshire Blvd.
Los Angeles, CA 90036

Tel: 323-931-1365
G. S. Hinsen Co.
2133 Bandywood Dr.
Nashville, TN 37215
Tel: 615-383-6440
Fax: 615-269-5130

Dakota Jackson
Dakota Jackson, Inc.
42-24 Orchard St. 5th Fl.
Long Island City, NY 11101
Tel: 718-786-8600

Charlotte Jensen & Associates
11464 Escoba Place
San Diego, CA 92127
Tel: 619-693-9294
Fax: 619-487-6895

Kanner Architects
10924 Le Conte Ave.
Los Angeles, CA 90024
Tel: 310-208-0028
Fax: 310-208-5756

Sandy Koepke Interior Design
1517 North Beverly Drive
Beverly Hills, CA 90210
Tel: 310-273-1960

Lake/Flato Architects, Inc.
311 3rd Street, Suite 200
San Antonio, TX 75205
Tel: 210-227-3335
Fax: 210-224-9515

Bill Lane
Bill Lane & Assoc., Inc.
926 North Orlando Ave.
Los Angeles, CA 90069
Tel: 310-657-7890

Luminaire
301 W. Superior Street
Chicago, IL 60610
Tel: 800-494-4358
or
2331 Ponce de Leon Blvd.
Coral Gables, FL 33134
Tel: 800-645-7250

Jeffrey Alan Marks
1040 West Muirlands Drive
La Jolla, CA 92037
Tel: 858-459-9192 or
310-207-2222

Donald Maxcy, ASID
Maxcy Design
P.O. Box 5507
Carmel, CA 93921
Tel: 408-625-5081
Fax: 408-625-5031

Linda Medina, ASID
3255 Talbot Street
San Diego, CA 92106

Frederick Miley Designs
345 Vermont
San Francisco, CA 94103
Tel: 415-931-5605
Fax: 415-626-9036

Benjamin Noriega-Ortiz
75 Spring Street
New York, NY 10012
Tel: 212-343-9709

Alan Ohashi
Ohashi Design Studio
5739 Presley Ave.
Berkeley, CA 94618
Tel: 510-652-8840
Fax: 510-652-8604

Lorcan O'Herlihy Architects
5709 Mesmer Avenue
Culver City, CA 90230
Tel: 323-931-1365

Pugh & Scarpa
Bergamot Station
2525 Michigan Ave.
Santa Monica, CA 90404
Tel: 310-828-0026

Andree Putman
83 Avenue Denfert Rochereau
Paris 75014
France

Priscillia Sanchez Interiors
444 De Haro Street
Suite 101
San Francisco, CA 94017
Tel: 415-864-7766
Fax: 415-864-1715

Sheperd Vineburg Designs
232 Fifth Place
Manhatten Beach, CA 90266
Tel: 310-318-6810

Ruth Soforenko & Assoc.
137 Forest Ave.
Palo Alto, CA 94301
Tel: 415-326-5448
Fax: 415-326-5539

Spiegel Catalog, Inc.
3500 Lacey Rd.
Downers Grove, IL 60515
Tel: 630-769-2591
Fax: 630-769-3686

Rysia Suchecka
NBBJ
111 South Jackson St.
Seattle, WA 98104
Tel: 206-223-5555

Jula Sutta
215 Crestview Dr
Orinda, CA 94563
Tel: 510-253-0862.

Yves Taralon
47 bis rue Bretagne
Paris 75003
France

Kelli Sue Tudor
Becker Zeyko U.S. Headquarters
1030 Marina Village Parkway
Almeda, CA 94501
Tel: 510-865-1616
Fax: 510-865-1148

Peter Wheeler
P.J. Wheeler Associates
47 Gray Street
Boston, MA 02116
Tel: 617-426-5921

Randall Whitehead, IALD, ASID
Light Source Design Group
1246 14th Street
San Francisco, CA 94107
Tel: 415-626-1210
Fax: 415-626-1821

York Wallcoverings
Ronald Redding
750 Linden Ave.
York, PA 17405-5166
Tel: 717-846-4456
Fax: 717-851-0409

DIRECTORY OF PHOTOGRAPHERS

Russell Abraham Photography
60 Federal Street
San Fransico, CA 94107
Tel: 415-896-6402
Fax: 415-896-6402

Dennis Anderson Photography
48 Lucky Drive
Greenbrae, CA 94904
Tel: 415-927-3530

B & B Italia, USA, Inc.
150 East 58th Street
New York, NY 10155

Roland Beaufre Photography
53 Ru Du Faubourg
Saint Antoine, Paris 75011
France
Tel: 33-1-53176394
Fax: 33-1-43409165

Tony Berardi
Photofields
36 W 830 Stonebridge Lane
St. Charles, IL 60175
Tel: 630-587-5530

Tom Bonner Photography
1201 Abbot Kinney Blvd.
Venice, CA 90291
Tel: 310-396-7125
Fax: 310-396-4792

Barbara Bouyea & Assoc.
3811 Turtle Creek Blvd., Suite 1010
Dallas, TX 75219
Tel: 214-520-6580
Fax: 214-520-6581

Jim Brady
Brady Architectural Photography
1010 University Ave.
San Diego, CA 92103
Tel: 619-296-5304
Fax: 619-296-5304

Michael Bruk Photographics
2205 Spaulding St.
Berkeley, CA 94703
Tel: 415-824-8600
Fax: 510-704-1933

Murray B. Brunswick
Brunschwig & Fils, Inc.
979 3rd Ave. Rm 1120
New York , NY 10022-1234
Tel: 212-838-7878
Fax: 212-371-3026

Beautriz Coll Photography
1715 9th St.
Berkeley, CA 94710
Tel: 510-526-2539

Grey Crawford Photography
2924 Park Center Dr.
Los Angeles, CA 90068
Tel: 213-413-4299
Fax: 323-851-4252

Mark Darley Photography
23 Midway Ave.
Mill Valley, CA 94941
Tel: 501-372-0640

Marylou Denny
2 Salt Creek Lane, Suite 114
Hindsdale, IL 60521
Tel: 630-323-0555
Fax: 630-323-1060

Mimi Drop
157 North Sycamore
Los Angeles, CA 90036
Tel: 213-857-0668

Karyn P. Erving
Imperial Wallcoverings
23645 Mercantiln Rd.
Cleveland, OH 44122
Tel: 216-464-3700

Scott Frances
Esto Photographics Inc.
222 Valley Place
Mamaroneck, NY 10543
Tel: 914-698-4060

Bill Geddes Photographer
215 West 78th Street
New York, NY 10024
Tel: 212-799-4464
Fax: 212-799-5576

David Glomb Photographer
71340 Estellita Drive
Ranch Mirage, CA 92270
Tel: 760-340-4455

Ed Gohlich Photography
Design Partners
P.O. Box 100919
Coponia, CA 92178
Tel: 619-423-4237

Sam Gray Photography
23 Westwood Road
Wellesley, MA 02482
Tel: 781-237-2711

Marianne Haas
28 Stadelhofersyrasse
Zurich-Chulmeigh
Switzerland
Tel: 8007-261-0904

Phillip Harvey Photography
911 Minna Street
San Francisco, CA 94103
Tel: 415-861-2188
Fax: 415-861-2091

G.S. Hinsen Company
2133 Bandywood Drive
Nashville, TN 37215
Tel: 615-383-6440
Fax: 615-269-5130

Lucie Hostalek & Grey Crawford
Beaute Works
2400 S Shenandoah St.
Los Angeles, CA 90034
Tel: 310-558-1100
Fax: 310-842-8889

Timothy Hursley Photography
1911 West Markham
Little Rock, AR 72205
Tel: 501-372-0640
Fax: 501-372-3366

Stephen Keating Photography
3603 33rd Ave. West
Seattle, WA 98199
Tel: 206-282-6506
Fax: 206-285-8709

Peter Margonelli
20 Debrosses Street
New York, NY 10013
Tel: 212-941-0380

Matthew Millman Photography
3127 Eton Ave.
Berkeley, CA 94705
Tel: 510-459-9030

Ira Montgomery Photography
2406 Converse
Dallas, TX 75201
Tel: 214-748-7288
Fax: 214-638-7980

Geralyn Lawson
Exposures
27 Ann Street
South Newark, CT 06854
Tel: 203-857-0027

David Duncun Livingston
1036 Erica Road
Mill Valley, CA 94941
Tel: 415-305-6050

Jeff McNamara
Austin Patterson Disston
376 Pequet Ave.
Southport, CT 06490
Tel: 203-255-4031
Fax: 203-254-1390

Mark Lohman Photography
1021 S. Fairfax Ave.
Los Angeles, CA 90019
Tel: 323-933-3359

Colin MacRae Photography
1061 Folsom Street
San Francisco, CA 94103
Tel: 415-863-0119
Fax: 415-558-0485

Mathew Millman Photography
821 Richmond Street
El Cemto, CA 94530
Tel: 510-459-9030
Fax: 510-526-1778

Mary E. Nichols
323 North Arden Blvd.
Los Angeles, CA 90004
Tel: 310-935-3080

Gill Nono
Nono Designs Ltd.
Craven Court
Altrincham WA14 SDY
United Kingdom
Tel: 161-929-9930
Fax: 161-929-9951

Peter R. Peirce Inc.
P.O. Box 662
Salisbury, CT 06068
Tel: 212-490-2646

Marvin Rand Associates
1310 Abbot Kinney Blvd.
Venice, CA 90291
Tel: 310-396-3441
Fax: 310-399-0298

Kenneth Rice Photography
456 61st Street
Oakland, CA 94609
Tel: 510-652-1752
Fax: 510-658-4355

Eric A. Roth
Henderson Studio
337 Summer Street
Boston, MA 02210

Bill Rothshild Photographer
19 Judith Lane
Wesley Hills, NY 10952
Tel: 212-752-3674

Jeremy Samuelson Photography
1188 South La Brea Ave.
Los Angeles, CA 90010
Tel: 213-937-5964
Fax: 213-937-6799

Ruth Soforenko Associates
137 Forest Ave.
Palo Alto, CA 94301
Tel: 415-326-5448
Fax: 415-326-5539

Monique Savarese
Dialogia
484 Broome Street
New York, NY 10013
Tel: 212-966-1934
Fax: 212-966-2870

Mikio Sekita
79 Leonard Street
New York, NY 10013

Tim Street-Porter
2074 Watsonia Terrace
Los Angeles, CA 90068
Tel: 323-874-4278

Steve Vierra Photography
P.O. Box 1827
Sandwich, MA 02563
Tel: 508-477-7043

Alan Weintraub Photography
1832 A Mason Street
San Francisco, CA 94114
Tel: 415-553-8191
Fax: 415-553-8192

Charles S. White
154 North Mansfield
Los Angeles, CA 90036
Tel: 213-937-3117

Toshi Yoshimi Photography
4030 Camero Ave.
Los Angeles, CA 90027
Tel: 323-660-9043
Fax: 323-660-2497

Eric A. Zepeda Photographer
1451 Stevenson St., Studio A
San Fransisco, CA 94103
Tel: 415-558-9691
Fax: 415-558-9681

ABOUT THE AUTHOR

Ann McArdle is a freelance writer who lives and works in Gloucester, Massachusetts. Recently retired from a career in publishing, she writes on a wide range of topics.

Her books on interior design include the series *Minimal Interiors*, *Romantic Interiors*, *Elegant Interiors*, and *Natural Interiors*, and *East-West Style*, all published by Rockport Publishers. Her book, *Stephanie's Angels*, will be appearing in 2000, published by Twin Lights Publishers.

In her free time, McArdle studies yoga and tutors at Gloucester's Wellspring House, Inc. in their Foundations Program teaching career skills to women in transition.